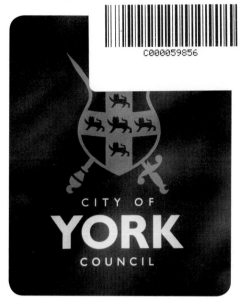

CITY OF
YORK
COUNCIL

The red cross of St George suggests the city's religious connections. The five gold lions passant of England emphasise its strong support of the English royal line.

*

Sometimes the arms are seen topped by a 'chapeau' – which represents the cap of maintenance worn by the bearer of the civic sword. This symbolic cap was first given to the city in 1393 by Richard II.

*

The coat of arms is often shown with the civic sword and mace behind it. These represent the city's powers of self-government under the mayor. A sword was given to the city by Richard II in 1387, which was allowed to be carried before the mayor on ceremonial occasions, and a charter in 1396 gave the right for a mace to be carried too.

Contents

What's in a Name?

Pronounced yawrk (jɔrk)

The original Celtic name was Eburos, or something similar. This has variously been translated as 'the estate of a man called Eburos' and 'yew tree' (a tree which was sacred to the Celts). The Romans corrupted this when they built their fortress there and recorded it as Eboracum (or Eburacum).

When the Anglo-Saxons settled here they called it Eoforwic, which translates as 'wild boar town' – from their word for wild boar, which was Eofor.

Then along came the Vikings, who referred to it as Jorvik, Norse for 'bay horse'.

Just Saying

'The extraordinary thing about York ... is that it's like an enormous trifle – wherever you dig, you discover amazing layers of history.'

Tony Robinson

'I was born in York and grew up there, so I have a great fondness for this remarkable city with its winding, cobbled streets and beautiful architecture. I have happy memories of my days at The Mount School... The city has evolved over the years, with the arrival of new and exciting attractions, a wealth of interesting shops and a vibrant café and evening culture. However, some things never change and, no matter how long I am away, that first glimpse of the magnificent Minster towering above the city will never cease to inspire and move me. I will always be proud to call York my home.'

Dame Judi Dench

'I was born in the year 1632, in the city of York, to a good family...'

The first line of *Robinson Crusoe* by Daniel Defoe

'York has England's finest set of medieval town churches. It has also been successful in bringing them back to life... They remain a wonderful complement to York Minster, evoking some sense of an English city in the late Middle Ages, each neighbourhood owing allegiance to an often tiny place of worship, enclosed by lanes and alleys.'

From *England's Thousand Best Churches* by Simon Jenkins

'Now is the winter of our discontent made glorious summer by this sun of York.'

***Richard III* by William Shakespeare**

'Off with his head and set it on York's gates; so York may overlook the Town of York.'

Queen Margaret in *Henry VI*, Part III by William Shakespeare

9

Walled Up

The most complete example of medieval city walls still standing in England are those you see in York.

The first fortifications were erected by the IX Roman Legion when they established their base in AD 71. They would have been constructed of earth ramparts with a timber palisade on top. This was replaced by a stone wall a little over 200 years later.

The Multangular Tower, which can still be seen in the Museum Gardens, had a twin at the other end of the wall, which is now buried underneath Feasegate. They were probably built in the reign of the Roman Emperor Septimius Severus.

The area inside the defences was huge, covering 20.3 hectares (50.16 acres).

The Vikings buried the Roman walls and reverted to using wooden palisades. Or did they? There seems to be some disagreement about York's walls during this period.

The thirteenth and fourteenth centuries saw the construction of the stone wall that is still there today.

The walls came in useful in 1644, during the English Civil War, when Royalist York was besieged by 30,000 of Cromwell's Roundheads.

Prince Rupert of the Rhine rode to the rescue on 1 July, only to be defeated at the Battle of Marston Moor on 2 July. The city surrendered on 16 July.

For a while in 1745 it looked like Bonnie Prince Charlie and his Jacobites might besiege York, but nothing came of that threat to the city.

The walls are still standing, despite the best efforts of the corporation to tear them down at the beginning of the nineteenth century. The Government of the day and the king soon put a stop to that.

Street Names

There are twenty-six 'gates' in York. These aren't gates in the modern sense of the word, but reminders of the city's Viking heritage: *gata* was Norse for a road or a way.

York's gates are:
Castlegate, Colliergate, Coppergate, Davygate, Feasegate, Fishergate, Fossgate, Gillygate, Goodramgate, Hosiergate, Hungate, Jubbergate, Marygate, Micklegate, Monkgate, Nessgate, Ousegate, Petergate, Skeldergate, Spurriergate, St Andrewgate, St Saviourgate, Stonegate, Swinegate, Walmgate and finally Whip-Ma-Whop-Ma-Gate.

Then there are the Bars – but you'd be disappointed if you popped in for a drink! These Bars are the city gates:

Bootham Bar, Micklegate Bar, Monk Bar and Walmgate Bar.

From 1501, these had door knockers fitted for 'Scots and other vagabonds and rascals' to rap on to gain entry!

Monk Bar retains its portcullis, which was last dropped in 1953 to celebrate the queen's coronation. Unfortunately, however, it plummeted to the ground when its ropes broke and ended up jammed in the road!

Probably the most well-known street in York is Shambles, which won the title of Britain's Most Picturesque Street in the Google Street View Awards 2010.

There are over fifty little alleyways – known as snickelways since 1983 when author Mark W. Jones coined the phrase. My personal favourite is Lund Court because it was formerly called Mad Alice Lane.

York in Numbers

York is one of only five urban areas that have been designated as Areas of Archaeological Importance (AAI) under the Ancient Monuments and Archaeological Areas Act (1979).There are seven AAIs in York. These include York City Centre and parts of Acomb, Dringhouses, Glen Road, Heworth, Middlethorpe and Retreat Area.

The Multangular Tower in Museum Gardens has nine sides and probably housed a catapult to fire at Anglo-Saxon invaders approaching the garrison from the river.

Thirteen Luddites were executed in York after being taken from Huddersfield to be tried and hanged in the city.

There are nineteen medieval churches still standing in York.

By 1900 there were twenty male urinals and three male WCs, but only one female WC in York city centre.

Over eighty skeletons, possibly gladiators, were discovered in a Roman cemetery on the outskirts of York.

The National Railway Museum has over 100 engines, interactive displays and exhibitions.

It is claimed that York has more than 500 ghosts floating round the city.

JORVIK Viking Centre includes among its exhibits 1,000-year-old timbers that once formed the wall of a Viking house.

From AD 71 there were 5,600 Roman soldiers in the city.

There are over 12,000 bed spaces in York.

Over 15,000 objects were recovered in the process of uncovering a Viking village complete with workshops, rubbish pits, latrines and wells.

The Nestlé UK archive at their York factory digitised over 37,000 photographs.

The population of York is 202,500 (1,600 of whom are over ninety years of age). This is made up of 98,600 men and 103,900 women.

Economically active: 91,269

Total Income Support claimants: 3,900

Ethnicity: 97.8 per cent white

York receives more than 7 million visitors each year.

13.5 million people have visited the JORVIK Viking Centre over the past twenty years.

Distance from York

	Km	Miles
St Paul's Cathedral, London	336	209
London Wall (Cooper's Row)	341	212
Notre Dame, Paris, France	777	483
The Pont Neuf, Paris, France	785	488
Saint-Benigne Cathedral, Dijon, France	10,062	660
Musee Archeologique, Dijon, France	10,062	660
Kiepenkerl Quarter, Münster	972	604
Westfälische Wilhelms-University, Münster	978	608
Smolny Cathedral, St Petersburg	3,032	1,884
Summer Palace, St Petersburg	3,045	1,892
Sydney Harbour Bridge, NSW, Australia	16,917	10,507
Sydney Opera House, NSW, Australia	16,930	10,520
St Patrick's Cathedral, New York, USA	5,598	3,479
Grand Central Station, New York, USA	5,431	3,378
The Ginza, Tokyo	9,465	5,881
Senso-ji Temple, Tokyo	9,474	5,887
Temple of Ten Thousand Buddhas, Hong Kong	9,634	5,986
The Peak, Hong Kong	9,626	5,982
Caffè Florian, Venice	1,848	1,148
St Mark's Basilica, Venice	1,848	1,148

Twinned Towns

York is twinned with two European towns, Dijon in France (since 1953) and Münster in Germany (since 1957).

Dijon is the historical capital of the Burgundy region – and there's a lot more to it than mustard! Reminiscent of York, its medieval history is apparent in its well-preserved Gothic cathedral and many other medieval buildings in the city's centre. The cathedral is dedicated to Saint Benignus, who is also Dijon's patron saint.

A city of culture, Dijon numbers orator and writer Bossuet and the composer Rameau among its native-born citizens. And Rousseau won fame after writing a prize-winning essay, *A Discourse on the Sciences and Arts*, for an Academy of Dijon competition.

There's plenty to see in Dijon, one of its distinguishing features being multi-coloured roof tiles forming geometric patterns. A really good view can be seen from the top of the 150ft-high Philippe Le Bon Tower at the Dukes of Burgundy Palace.

There are also plenty of museums – including the Museum of Mustard….

Situated in North Rhine-Westphalia, Münster is a regional capital in the north of its home country. With its medieval cathedral and market place, along with many historic buildings and museums, it has a lot in common with York.

Its city status was granted in 805, but Münster traces its history back to AD 793 and the founding of a monastery here. Münster has a university – the third largest in Germany. This is situated in the schloss, or castle, which lies just outside the western edge of the Altstadt.

Münster describes itself as the 'City of Sculptures' and has fifty-seven major works scattered about the city.

Historical Timeline

King Edwin of Northumbria was baptised in York by Paulinus, York's first Bishop

William the Conqueror arrived in York and built the first castle

Edward I moved the Chancery and Exchequer to York, effectively making the city England's capital, albeit briefly

Civil War siege of York

Jonathan Martin set the quire of York Minster on fire, causing a huge amount of damage

The Romans founded York

Vikings captured the city

AD 71   627   866   1068   1298   1644   1829

306   732   1066   1190   1328   1739   1830

Constantine proclaimed Emperor in York

York had a population of about 9,000 or 10,000

King Edward III married Philippa of Hainault in York Minster

Official opening of new premises for Yorkshire Museum, founded by the Yorkshire Philosophical Society in 1828

Egbert became the first Archbishop of York

Massacre of Jews who had taken refuge in the castle

The highwayman Dick Turpin hanged at York racecourse for sheep and horse theft

The first railway arrived

1839

1840 — Another fire in York Minster destroyed the nave, roof and vault

Rowntree's confectionary company founded

1862

1920s — York Council began carrying out slum clearances to make way for new council houses

The Germans bombed York: ninety-two people killed and historic buildings damaged

1942

The entire historic core of York designated a conservation area

1968

1963 — York University founded

National Railway Museum opened

1975

ARC (Archaeological Resource Centre) opened

Damage to the Minster took four years to repair after yet another fire

1984

York Racecourse hosted Royal Ascot during the latter's refurbishment

2005

1990 — York voted 'European Tourism City of the Year' by European Cities Marketing

University of York named 'University of the Year' at *The Times* Higher Education Awards

2010

2007

Other Yorks

In the USA there are seventeen towns and villages called York (New York City, counties and unpopulated areas have not been included). These can be found in the following states:

Alabama, Georgia, Illinois, Indiana, Iowa, Kentucky, Michigan, Minnesota, Missouri, Montana, Nebraska, New York, North Dakota, Ohio, Pennsylvania, South Carolina, Wisconsin.

York, Indiana. There are six towns in Indiana with the name of York.

York, Nebraska is within a few miles of the geographical centre of the United States.

York, Pennsylvania was the first capital of the United States and birthplace of the Articles of Confederation. The designation 'The United States' was used for the first time here.

York, South Carolina is USA's fifth largest York.

And in other countries:
Western Australia

The first inland European settlement in Western Australia, settlers reached Australian York on 15 September 1831. It is now a tourist town and hosts numerous festivals and events – just like its namesake.

Sierra Leone

York is a small Creole fishing village on the Freetown Peninsula.

York's 800th Anniversary

On 9 July 1212 King John granted York a Royal Charter, which made York a self-governing city that could collect taxes and trade freely. It also allowed the mayor and council to be elected by the citizens. But this privilege didn't come cheap; in return, John was paid £200 and three horses.

York's first mayor was Hugh Selby, who exported wool to the Low Countries and imported wine from Anjou. He and his family held the office so many times between them (seventeen) that the post could almost be considered a 'family business'! Today, the Lord Mayor of York is second only to the Lord Mayor of London, in terms of precedence. There's still a Sheriff of York, this particular office being the oldest in England and Wales. However, Henry III deprived the official of his powers in 1256, so that law and justice was then in the hands of the people of York.

800 years later a modern monarch, Queen Elizabeth II, visited the city in her Diamond Jubilee year to support York in its own special celebrations. Events celebrating the 800th anniversary were organised to cover the whole year, with community choirs performing a specially composed piece on Charter Day itself.

Festivals

Every year York hosts more than thirty different festivals. The year starts with Holocaust Memorial Day in January and ends with the Festival of Angels in mid-December. Whatever your interest, York probably has it covered:

Jorvik Viking Festival

In a way, this festival is over 1,000 years old. The Vikings used to put on a festival each year in February, celebrating the end of winter's hardships and the arrival of spring. It was revived in 1985, making it one of York's oldest modern festivals – maybe even the oldest. And it's still held every February.

York Chocolate Festival

Definitely not a festival for dieters! There's a Chocolate Market, demonstrations, tastings and workshops. There are chocolate-related tours, challenges and hunts that finish with chocolate treats. And you also get free samples!

Illuminating York

See York in a new light! This annual autumn digital arts and lighting festival bathes many of York's buildings in spectacular lighting displays.

Other festivals include:

York Residents Festival

York Festival of Fairtrade

Festival of Storytelling

Festival of Science & Technology

York Literature Festival

Festival of Writing

Fashion City York

York Open Studios

Spring Festival of New Music

York Carnival

York Cycle Show

York Roman Festival

York Early Music Festival

Festival of Youth

York Festival of the Rivers

York Festival of Traditional Dance

Peace Festival

York National Book Fair

York Food & Drink Festival

CAMRA Beer & Cider Festival

Railfest

York 50+ Festival

York Ghost Festival

Aesthetica Short Film Festival

Interfaith Week

York Early Music Christmas Festival

St Nicholas Fayre

Freak Weather

1881
In mid-January York's maximum temperature was -7.8C.

1945
Freezing fog resulted in a Halifax bomber icing up so badly that it crashed onto a York suburb just 1.5 miles south of York Minster. Most of the crew and five civilians were killed and eighteen people were injured.

1947
This year was such a severe winter throughout the whole country that nobody who experienced it would ever forget it: the conditions were glacial. When the heavy snowfall melted in March, over 2,000 houses on the Tang Hall Estate, 1.5 miles east of York Minster, were flooded.

1979
So much snow fell that the York to Beverley road was impassable.

1980
It snowed in June.

1984
North Yorkshire's Fire Brigade suspected that it was a lightning strike which caused the fire that destroyed the roof and the South Transept of York Minster. The blaze shattered the fifteenth-century rose window.

2000
York station was hit by lightning four times in the space of a few minutes, knocking out signalling systems and halting all trains for half an hour.

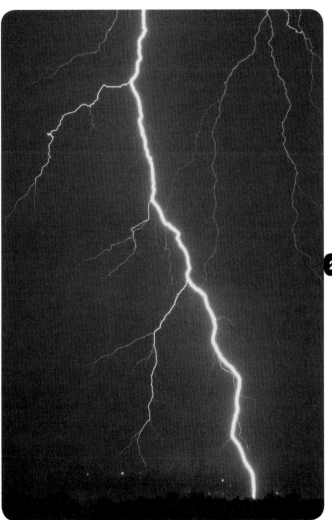

Floods

York's bit of the River Ouse seems to flood at the drop of a hat.

1564
Heavy snow falls followed by thaws resulted in floods which caused the Ouse Bridge to collapse. A dozen houses built on the bridge crumpled into the river, together with their unfortunate inhabitants.

1877
Floodwaters reached over 13ft above the river's normal level, damaging local houses.

1892
The river rose 11ft higher than its usual level, causing the sewage works to flood.

1968
Heavy rains in the Dales caused the Ouse to flood in York.

1991
The river reached its highest level of the twentieth century, but worse was to follow in the next millennium.

2000
In the autumn, York was hit by some of the worst floods in its history when the Ouse burst its banks once again. Hundreds of residents were affected and it cost the City Council £1.3 million to deal with it.

Dukes of York

The title is usually given to the monarch's second son, Prince Andrew being created Duke of York in 1986. The title can be inherited, but never has been because the titleholder has either died without producing a male heir, or has become king himself.

The present Duke of York was the first child to be born to a reigning monarch for 103 years. He served for twenty-two years in the Royal Navy as a helicopter pilot.

Other title holders include:
Edmund of Langley, for whom the title was created in 1385. He was the founder of the House of York.

Sir Edward of Norwich, who died at the Battle of Agincourt – he fell off his horse and suffocated beneath a heap of other men and horses.

Richard Plantagenet became Regent and Protector of the Realm in 1454 during a period when Henry VI was incapacitated due to a mental health problem.

King Edward IV was the first Yorkist king of England and at approximately 9.93m (6ft 4in) is the tallest British monarch in our history so far.

Richard of Shrewsbury was one of the Princes in the Tower, allegedly murdered by Richard III.

Henry VIII was made Duke of York in 1494, aged just three.

James Stuart, the second son of Charles I, had New York named in his honour.

Prince Albert, the present queen's father, became George VI when his brother (Edward VIII) abdicated.

A Nursery Rhyme

The Grand old Duke of York he had ten thousand men
He marched them up to the top of the hill
And he marched them down again.
When they were up, they were up
And when they were down, they were down
And when they were only halfway up
They were neither up nor down.

It's not at all clear which Duke of York is being referred to in the nursery rhyme. In fact, originally it may even have referred to a king of France and not to a Duke of York at all. Contenders in the Duke of York stakes include:

Richard, Duke of York (1411-1460), father of Edward IV and Richard III

James II (1633-1701), formerly Duke of York

Prince Frederick, Duke of York and Albany (1763-1827), the second son of King George III

FREDERICK
DUKE OF YORK
1763 — 1827
Second Son of George III
Commander-in-Chief
of the British Army
1795-1809 and 1811-1827

Famous for ...

York Minster is the most visited cathedral in Britain. Its full title is 'The Cathedral and Metropolitical Church of St Peter in York'.

The Minster stands above the site of the Roman headquarters.

The first church on this site was a wooden one, built for the baptism of the Anglo-Saxon King Edwin of Northumbria, which took place on Easter Sunday AD 627.

The present church took 252 years to complete, being finished in 1472.

The oldest part of the Minster visible above ground is the south transept.

It is built from magnesian limestone, which comes from Yorkshire quarries.

The building is over 500ft long and 100ft wide; its central tower is 200ft high.

275 stairs lead to the top of the central tower, which weighs 16,000 tonnes.

There are 128 windows, containing about 2 million individual pieces of glass. Each window is cleaned and restored every 125 years.

The Great East Window is the largest medieval stained-glass window in Britain and is the size of a tennis court.

The oldest carvings can be found on the walls of the octagonal Chapter House.

The astronomical clock is an unusual war memorial which was installed in 1955 to honour airmen based in Yorkshire, Durham, and Northumberland killed in action during the Second World War.

Edward III was married in York Minster in 1328 to Philippa of Hainault. Prince William of Hatfield, a son who died when he was only ten years old, is buried here.

Infamous for...

The massacre of the Jewish population of York on 16 March 1190.

Two of York's leading Jews had travelled to London to present gifts to Richard I on the occasion of his coronation, despite the fact England's Jewish community had been barred from attending the event. The crowd that had gathered at Westminster saw this as an insult and one of the pair was wounded in the ensuing fracas, dying from his wounds on his way home to York. Six months later, a mob broke into his house and murdered his widow and children.

The frightened Jewish community of about 150 people sought refuge in the wooden castle where Clifford's Tower now stands. Believing they would either be murdered by the angry mob outside or forced to be baptised, many of them chose suicide. A few believed promises of mercy, but were slain next morning when they left the safety of the castle.

York's citizens had to pay a substantial fine as punishment and both the sheriff and constable were dismissed.

In December 1978 a memorial plaque was placed at the site.

York's Oldest...

...city gate is Bootham Bar

...street is Shambles, already in existence by the time of the Domesday survey

...house is a twelfth-century restored Norman residence; it's up an alley between Nos 50 and 52 Stonegate

...church is St Mary's Bishophill Junior, parts of the tower dating back to the eleventh century

...non-conformist church is St Saviourgate Unitarian Chapel, dating from 1693

...school is St Peter's, which was established in AD 627

...pub: there are two rival claimants, The Olde Starre Inn and The Golden Fleece

...glass is in a window in York Minster; dating back to the middle of the twelfth century, it is thought to be the oldest glass in England

...existing horticultural society is The Ancient Society of York Florists, whose records date back to 1768 (when florists grew their own flowers for exhibition purposes)

But predating all of them by a very long way is:

...a 2,000-year-old brain which was found during an excavation of York University's campus in 2008!

Archbishops of York

Paulinus was the first Bishop of York (627–633). He never actually received the vestments (the pallium), sent to him by Pope Honorius, which would have made him Archbishop.

Ecgbeorht, or Egbert, is considered the first true Archbishop of York. He was in post for over thirty years.

Two Archbishops have served for even longer: both Walter de Grey (thirteenth century) and Edward Harcourt (nineteenth century) were Archbishops for forty years.

William Fitzherbert was Archbishop twice, first from 1143 to 1147 and again in 1153/1154. He was made a saint and is now York's patron saint.

Richard le Scrope was Archbishop for nearly nine years, from 1398, but made the mistake of leading an uprising against the king and was beheaded in a field near Skeldergate.

Cardinal Thomas Wolsey began his term of office in 1514, but never spent so much as an hour in York in all his sixteen years of service.

Lancelot Blackburne was Archbishop of York 1724-1743. Rumour has it he was a pirate for a while, but there's no real proof. Walpole also considered him a ladies' man!

At the time of writing, the present Archbishop is Dr John Sentamu, who took office in 2005.

1181 Geoffrey Plantagenet	1660 Accepted Frewen
1215 Walter de Gray	1664 Richard Sterne
1256 Sewal de Bovill	1683 John Dolben
1258 Godfrey of Ludham	1688 Thomas Lamplugh
1266 Walter Giffard	1691 John Sharp
1279 William Wickwane	1714 Sir William Dawes
1286 John Le Romeyn	1724 Lancelot Blackburne
1298 Henry of Newark	1743 Thomas Herring
1300 Thomas of Corbridge	1747 Matthew Hutton
1306 William Greenfield	1757 John Gilbert
1317 William of Melton	1761 Robert Hay Drummond
1342 William La Zouche	1777 William Markham
1352 John of Thoresby	1807 Edward Vernon-Harcourt
1374 Alexander Neville	1847 Thomas Musgrave
1388 Thomas Arundel	1860 Charles Longley
1396 Robert Waldby	1862 William Thomson
1398 Richard Le Scrope	1890 William Magee
1407 Henry Bowet	1891 William Maclagan
1425 John Kempe	1909 Cosmo Gordon Lang
1452 William Booth	1928 William Temple
1465 George Neville	1942 Cyril Forster Garbett
1476 Lawrence Booth	1956 Michael Ramsey
1480 Thomas Rotherham	1961 Donald Coggan
1501 Thomas Savage	1975 Stuart Blanch
1508 Christopher Bainbridge	1983 John Habgood
1514 Thomas Wolsey	1995 David Hope
1531 Edward Lee	2005 John Sentamu
1545 Robert Holgate	
1555 Nicholas Heath	
1561 Thomas Young	
1570 Edmund Grindal	
1577 Edwin Sandys	
1589 John Piers	
1595 Matthew Hutton	
1606 Tobias Matthew	
1628 George Monteigne	
1628 Samuel Harsnett	
1632 Richard Neile	
1641 John Williams	In memory of Arthur Michael Ramsey

43

Saint William: Patron Saint of York

William Fitzherbert became Archbishop of York for the first time in 1143 against a background of controversy. The Cistercians, who wanted their own candidate for the post, said he was 'rotten from the soles of his feet to the crown of his head'. The Pope deposed William in 1147, replacing him with Henry Murdac, Abbot of the Cistercian Fountains Abbey. However, when he tried to enter York the following year the residents refused to let him in!

In 1153, both Murdac and the Pope died and William was restored to the See of York. A large crowd turned out to welcome him, many of them standing on Ouse Bridge – which promptly collapsed under their weight. William called on God to save those who were in danger of drowning. Nobody died, which is seen as his first miracle.

In June 1154, William celebrated Mass in York Minster, but fell ill and died a week later. The earliest of the miracles attributed to him following his death recounts how the Minster caught fire and a heavy burning beam crashed onto his tomb, breaking its cover. William's body became visible in its silk vestments, but neither his corpse nor his clothing was so much as singed.

Thirty-three further miracles were recorded, all of them taking place at his tomb. These included curing the crippled, the blind, the deaf and 'the humpbacked'. Stomach ailments were also on the list of cures, one of which is particularly interesting. A frog had accidentally been cooked in some bread which a lady ate; she subsequently suffered two years of terrible stomach pains and sickness. A visit to St William's tomb soon cured her, though.

William was canonised by Pope Honorius III on 18 March 1226 and his festival is observed on 8 June.

Flora

York roses include: 'City of York' and 'Duke of York'

Iris latifolia 'Duchess of York'

Narcissus 'York Minster'

Pelargonium 'York Minster'

Primula auricula 'Duchess of York'

Prunus persica 'Duke of York'

Sambucus nigra subsp. canadensis 'York'

47

A Hidden Jewel

Just 2 miles south-west of York Minster, there's another jewel in York's crown – The Yorkshire Wildlife Trust's nature reserve at Askham Bog.

Originally known as the Yorkshire Naturalists' Trust, the Trust was formed in 1946 and is part of a network of forty-seven individual Wildlife Trusts covering the whole of the UK. It procured Askham Bog, its first acquisition, the same year that the Trust was formed. It now manages over eighty-five nature reserves across Yorkshire.

We have the banker Charles Rothschild to thank for all this. He envisioned a plan to identify and protect areas for wildlife and established The Society for the Promotion of Nature Reserves in 1912 to achieve that aim. A century later and his vision has proved itself a thriving reality.

The boardwalk in this lovely nature reserve makes it accessible to everyone: pram pushers, those in wheelchairs, those using their own two feet. Sitting in a peat-filled ancient lake basin, this mix of fen, bog, grassland and woodland is home to a variety of plants, insects, birds and animals, some of them rare. Here, among many other delights, you can see:

Gingerbread sedge, marsh and common orchids, and meadow thistle (almost its most northerly site)

Brimstone butterflies, fen square-spot moth, and southern hawker dragonflies

Grasshopper warblers, tree creepers, and goshawks

Water voles, roe deer and foxes

There are even Exmoor ponies, which do a great job of preventing bushes and trees spreading into areas that have been painstakingly cleared by human volunteers.

Hangman

From the fourteenth century until 1800, public hangings in York were carried out on Knavesmire. Then a new gallows was erected inside the castle in 1800. Convicted men were chosen to act as hangmen, which earned them a reprieve if they were under a death sentence themselves.

Thomas Hadfield, sentenced to death for highway robbery, escaped death himself by becoming the hangman who executed Dick Turpin at Knavesmore on 7 April 1739. Apparently the pair of them chatted and joked for half an hour before the deed was done. One imagines that they had a lot in common to talk about!

William 'Mutton' Curry (aka William Wilkinson) had been convicted for theft of sheep. He started his new career in 1802 and stayed in the job until 1835. He'd been awaiting transportation to Australia when the vacancy cropped up. He was sentenced to death twice for his crimes, but each time the sentence was commuted to transportation. Although he held the job for thirty-three years, he tended to hit the bottle, which caused him to make a mess of some of his hangings.

James Coates only carried out two hangings before escaping from jail altogether. He was never re-captured.

Nathanial Howard was a coal-porter, not a convict, and was sixty when he took the job on from 1840 to 1853. He executed eleven people.

The last York hangman was Thomas Askern, who took over the office in 1856; he had been jailed for debt. His first hanging was carried out in front of an audience of 20,000.

After 1878, hangmen were expected to work countrywide.

THE
TRIAL

Of the Notorious Highwayman

𝕽𝖎𝖈𝖍𝖆𝖗𝖉 𝕿𝖚𝖗𝖕𝖎𝖓,

At *York* Aſſizes, on the 22d Day of *March*, 1739, before the Hon. Sir WILLIAM CHAPPLE, Kt. Judge of Aſſize, and one of His Majeſty's Juſtices of the Court of King's Bench.

Taken down in Court by Mr. THOMAS KYLL, Profeſſor of Short Hand.

To which is prefix'd,

An exact Account of the ſaid *Turpin*, from his firſt coming into *Yorkſhire*, to the Time of his being committed Priſoner to *York* Caſtle; communicated by Mr. APPLETON of *Beverley*, Clerk of the Peace for the *Eaſt-Riding* of the ſaid County.

With a Copy of a Letter which *Turpin* received from his Father, while under Sentence of Death.

To which is added,

His Behaviour at the Place of Execution, on *Saturday* the 7th of *April*, 1739. Together with the whole Confeſſion he made to the Hangman at the Gallows; wherein he acknowledg'd himſelf guilty of the Facts for which he ſuffer'd, own'd the Murder of Mr. *Thompſon*'s Servant on *Epping-Foreſt*, and gave a particular Account of ſeveral Robberies which he had committed.

YORK:

Printed by WARD and CHANDLER; and Sold at their Shop without *Temple-Bar*, *London*; and in *Coney-Street*, *York*, 1739.   (Price Six-pence.)

Star Track

If you want to head off to the solar system, grab yourself a bike – the planets are a lot closer than you think! A 10km (6.4 miles) long scale model of the solar system can be found on part of the White Rose cycle path on the outskirts of York.

The scale of the model is 575,872,239 to 1.

Each 100m (109 yards) along the cycle path equals over 57 million km (35.5 million miles) in space.

The first star you'll encounter is the Sun, in the form of a 2.4m (8ft) golden globe suspended above the path.

As you travel further, you'll encounter scale models of all the planets, with information shown for each of them. Remember, everything is to scale.

The route covers part of the diverted East Coast main-line railway.

Sustran bought the land and took six months to construct the model. It was the first venture for this leading UK charity which pioneered the concept of 'Safe Routes' throughout the UK. They have also created the National Cycle Network.

There's no need to get hungry or thirsty on your journey through the solar system. There's a supermarket at one end of the route and a village with shops and pubs at the other. In between, you can stop for a cuppa at the old Naburn Station café.

Bikes can be hired in York.

And finally, whether you are on foot or on two wheels, you can move faster than the speed of light here! The speed of light at this scale is about 1.16mph; the average walking speed is about 4mph (depending on age and health, of course) and a cyclist will pedal much more quickly than that.

Rebellion and Protest

'Remember, remember the 5th of November' (1605) –
for three of the Gunpowder plotters were from York:
Guy Fawkes, Christopher Wright and John Wright.

The trio attended St Peter's School in York.

Guy was born in 1570 and baptised in the church of St
Michael le Belfrey on 16 April: a plaque on the wall at this
church commemorates this. He was eight years old when
his father died; his mother subsequently remarried into a
Catholic family. Guy had been brought up as a Protestant,
but became a convert to the Catholic faith. In 1593 Fawkes
went to the Netherlands, enlisted in the Spanish army and
helped the Spanish capture Calais in 1596. He then travelled
to Spain where he tried to persuade King Philip II to invade
England. Although a minor character in the plot to blow up
Parliament and kill King James I, he was sentenced to death.
However, he jumped from the ladder on his way up to the
scaffold, broke his neck and died before he could be hanged.
He was quartered anyway and his body parts distributed
around the kingdom as a warning to other potential traitors.

The custom of celebrating a monarch's accession by lighting
bonfires was incorporated into law by King James I, the
celebration to take place each 5 November. Although that
law was repealed in 1859, we still celebrate Bonfire Night.

The first York rebels showed up much earlier than that.
In 1069 William the Conqueror destroyed a section of the
city so that he could build another castle there. The city's
inhabitants retaliated by burning down both castles and
slaughtering the occupants.

On July 1537 a gallows was built outside Clifford's Tower
and Robert Aske was hanged on it, in chains, for treason.
He was a lawyer from Selby who led the Pilgrimage of Grace
and occupied York on 16 October 1536.

Holgate Windmill

At one time York was surrounded by windmills, but now there's just one. It no longer stands in unspoilt countryside, but in the middle of a housing estate.

Holgate Mill is one of only two working mills in Yorkshire.

It is Grade II listed.

The mill was built in 1770 and continued to do its job as a corn mill until the 1930s.

The first miller was George Waud or Ward and the last was Thomas Mollet.

It is a five-storey tower mill comprising the ground floor, stone floor, bin floor, hoist floor, and cap or dust floor.

2001 saw the formation of the Holgate Preservation Society.

Five new sails were fitted on 20 December 2011.

There are Open Days each year.

Roman Baths

A pub and the council's new HQ have something in common: Roman baths have been found in both locations.

The Roman Bath public house was being renovated in 1930 when a semi-circular bath, part of the caldarium of the legionary baths, was found which dated back to the fourth century.

Tiles from the time of the VI and IX Legions have been re-used in building this bath and the masonry is comparable to that of the Multangular Tower in the Yorkshire Museum gardens.

The pub has turned the bath area into a little museum which is open 11 a.m. – 4.p.m every day except Christmas Day.

The bath complex excavated at the council's new HQ site dates from the second and third centuries.

These baths were used by the city's inhabitants, as the Roman army's baths were across the river.

First discovered in the 1840s during the building of York's original railway station, the latest finds were excavated in 2011.

Walks

There are sightseeing buses which will take tourists round York, but it's a city that is really best seen on foot. It's possible to walk along York's castle walls, which will give you a real feel for the history of the place, not to mention some splendid views. You don't have to walk the full 3.4km (2 miles) – there are plenty of places to get on and off.

A nice 3.4km (2 miles) walk along the river, created in the eighteenth century, starts opposite Clifford's Tower. Known as New Walk, the section of walk on the York side of the river was created in the 1730s, during the reign of George II.

It was part of the council's effort to promote the city as a fashionable place to live; somewhere for the local elite to walk and socialise with those of a similar status in life. When the Millennium Bridge was opened in 2001, it became possible to cross the river and return to the city on the opposite bank. You will pass the 30-acre Rowntree Park if you choose to return that way – somewhere to either rest, or extend your walk.

There are also lots of walks, some of them free, led by experienced guides. Details can be found at the Visitor Information Centre on Museum Street (not far from the Minster). You can meander through various aspects of the city's history and heritage, or explore the haunts of the many ghosts that populate 'Europe's Most Haunted City' (according to the International Ghost Research Foundation).

After a trip round the local brewery, you may well be glad to go on the tour of York's historic toilets!

Nature Reserves

Acomb Wood and Meadow Local Nature Reserve are 10 acres of mixed woodland and ancient meadow. The evidence hints at both previous planting of trees and use as arable land.

Across Acomb Wood Drive is the Woodland Trust's West Wood which has some uncommon flowers in it.

Clifton Backies Local Nature Reserve is situated between Bootham Stray and Water Lane in Clifton Without.

Hob Moor Local Nature Reserve is between Thanet Road and to the west of Tadcaster Road. Skylarks and meadow pipets, which are endangered species in the United Kingdom, both breed here.

St Nicholas Fields Local Nature Reserve in Tang Hall is a reclaimed area which is developing habitats including meadows and woodland.

63

Some Facts About York

The commander of the Roman legion that founded York in AD 71 was Petilius Cerialis.

In 1069 the Normans accidentally burnt down most of York, including the Minster. They only intended to destroy the houses close to the castle as a defensive measure, but the flames got out of hand.

The Ouse Bridge has the dubious distinction of conveniently housing the first public toilet in Yorkshire, back in 1367. It may even have been the first public loo in the country.

York Minster has its own police force.

Clifford's Tower was named after Roger de Clifford, who was hanged there on 23 March 1322 for his part in a rebellion against King Edward II's favourite, Hugh Le Despenser – in essence, he was opposing the king.

George Fox, founder of the Society of Friends, was thrown down the steps of York Minster by the congregation when he decided to preach to them after the sermon.

York Minster Outside

York Minster Inside

10818. - YORK MINSTER CHOIR EAST.

From the City Walls,
Then & Now

Turner in York

The great artist J.M.W. Turner RA (23 April 1775 –
19 December 1851) visited Yorkshire many times, often
staying with his friend and patron Walter Fawkes at his
Farnley Hall home.

Turner was twenty-two when he first travelled north in
1775, and he returned here throughout his life, visiting and
painting or sketching in over seventy locations.

He came to York on several occasions and, like so many
visitors today, he went to York Minster – where he carried
out five sketches inside the great church. He also painted a
watercolour from the River Ouse, showing it in the distance
with the river leading the eye towards the great building.

He sketched the ruins of St Mary's Abbey twice, producing a
beautifully detailed drawing of the west portal and another
more general view of the ruins.

He also made a number of sketches of the Ouse Bridge
from various angles – though the bridge Turner drew was
an earlier one than that which spans the river today. His
bridge was demolished in 1810, the present one being
completed in 1821.

Micklegate Bar, Then & Now

Scientists

Martin Lister (1639–1712) practised in York from 1670 to 1683 and was Queen Anne's physician. He is also credited with being the first to realise the importance of geological survey maps.

John Burton (1710–1771) invented obstetric forceps. He practiced in York as a doctor and male midwife. He was instrumental in establishing the York County Hospital in 1740.

John Goodricke (1764–86), mathematician and astronomer; he was living in York when he discovered the binary star Algol (Beta Persei) in 1782. He also discovered and calibrated the variable brightness of stars.

Thomas Cooke (1807–1868), an instrument maker, established his business in 1837. He founded T. Cooke & Sons, which later supplied six theodolites made for Scott's 1912 Antarctic Expedition.

John Snow (1813–1858) was born in York in 1813 and was a pioneer in anaesthesia. He was also one of the founders of modern epidemiology, recognising that cholera was caused by a germ. The University of York continues Snow's work: in 2012, a team of biologists from the university made a significant advance in understanding how cholera attacks the body.

Rivers, Lakes and Ponds

The River Ouse is about 84km (52 miles) long and drains into the Humber Estuary. It runs for approximately 21km (13 miles) through York, stretching from the Parish of Nether Poppleton in the north to Naburn in the south. It is England's sixth longest river.

The River Foss is about 27km (17 miles) long and has its source beside Oulston Reservoir near Newburgh Prior. It once formed a pond stretching for over 1.6km (1 mile) between Hungate, near the centre of York, and Layerthorpe. It used to be referred to as 'The King's Fishpond' or 'The King's Pool'.

Rawcliffe Lake is a shallow, man-made lake which lies in the middle of a housing estate in a north-western suburb of the city. It is available for fishing (rod licence needed) and is stocked with roach, bream, carp, tench and chub.

Chapman's Pond, in a suburb to the south-west of the city, is a former clay working surrounded by grassland and scrub woodland. Well stocked with a variety of coarse fish, it is managed by The Friends of Chapman's Pond.

Famous People (Modern)

Dame Judi Dench attended the city's Mount School. At the time of writing she has won thirty-five awards for her film, television and theatre work, including an Oscar for Best Supporting Actress for her performance in *Shakespeare in Love* and a Golden Globe for Best Actress in *The Last of the Blonde Bombshells*. She was also awarded a BAFTA Academy Fellowship and a Society of London Theatre Special Award.

John Barry composed twelve soundtracks for the Bond films and won Academy Awards for his music in *Born Free, The Lion In Winter, Out Of Africa* and *Dances With Wolves*. He also won Grammy awards for *Midnight Cowboy* and *The Cotton Club*.

W.H. Auden, the poet, was born in York, although his family then moved to Birmingham. His poem *Funeral Blues* was used in *Four Weddings and a Funeral*.

Anita Lonsbrough, MBE, was born in York; this swimmer won a gold medal at the 1960 Summer Olympics.

Kate Atkinson won the Whitbread Book of the Year prize in 1995 with the family saga *Behind the Scenes at the Museum*, which was set in York.

Frankie Howerd, OBE, born in York, was a comedian and comic actor. Probably best remembered for his role as Lurcio in the television series *Up Pompeii!,* he also starred in seventeen films, including *The Ladykillers* and *The Great St Trinian's Train Robbery*.

Dr 'Vince' Cable, a Liberal Democrat politician, economist and Business Secretary, was born and educated in York.

David Bradley, as well as acting in theatre and on television, also played Argus Filch in the *Harry Potter* series.

Mark Addy, born in Tang Hall, York, is a television and film actor who played Dave in *The Full Monty* and Fred Flintstone in *Flintstones in Las Vegas*.

Famous People (Historical)

Constantine the Great (*c.* 274–337), declared Emperor in York in AD 306, was the only Roman emperor to have been crowned anywhere outside of Rome.

Alcuin (*c.* 735–804) was an Anglo-Saxon scholar educated at York's cathedral school in around AD 750. He was one of Charlemagne's chief advisers on religious and educational matters.

Eric Bloodaxe (?–954) was briefly king of York and Northumbria. His death, in AD 954, ended independent Viking rule in Northumbria.

Guy Fawkes (1570–1606) attended York's St Peter's School with John and Christopher Wright, co-conspirators in the Gunpowder Plot of 1605. He was tried for treason at Westminster.

Dick Turpin (1705–1739) was born in Essex. This murderer and thief fled to Yorkshire to evade capture, but was caught and hanged in York in 1739.

William Etty (1787–1849) was a controversial artist born in York in 1787. He returned here shortly before his death.

Joseph Hansom (1803–1882) was born in York in 1803 and is best known as the inventor of the Hansom cab.

Joseph Rowntree (1836–1925) was a philanthropist born in York in 1836. He established a confectionary business with his brother.

Sir Joseph Barnby (1838–1896) was a musical composer and conductor born in York.

Mr Tempest Anderson (1846–1913) had a day job as an ophthalmic surgeon at York County Hospital, but he was also one of the pioneers of modern volcanology.

Educated in York

A.S. Byatt (Dame Antonia Duffy) is a prolific author, and winner of the Booker Prize for her novel *Possession: A Romance*. She attended The Mount School in York. Among her many other works are *Ragnarok: The End of the Gods* and *A Whistling Woman*.

Dame Margaret Drabble also attended The Mount School in York and is the author of seventeen novels, including *The Red Queen* and *The Sea Lady*. Her non-fiction work includes *Angus Wilson: A Biography* and *For Queen and Country: Britain in the Victorian Age*.

Jung Chang, the author of the award-winning book *Wild Swans*, studied at York University.

Graham Swift won the 1996 Booker prize with *Last Orders*. He attended York University.

Greg Dyke, the former Director-General of the BBC, graduated with a degree in politics from York University.

Harry Enfield, the well-known comedian, read politics at York University.

James Callis, the actor, read English and Related Literature at York University. His work includes appearances in *Midsomer Murders, Merlin, FlashForward, Battlestar Galactica* and *Soldier Soldier*.

A Saintly Educator

St Alcuin (*c.*735–804)

Alcuin was probably born in or near York. He became headmaster of York's cathedral school in 778 after being both a pupil and teacher there.

He taught there for fifteen years, and under his guidance the school became internationally famous both for its library and its teaching in the liberal arts, literature and science – as well as in religious matters.

He went on to act as adviser to Charlemagne on religious and educational matters.

Later, Alcuin became head of the Palace School at Aachen before being made abbot of St Martin's Monastery at Tours at the age of sixty, founding a school and library there and attracting scholars from all over Europe.

Known during his lifetime for his holiness and scholarly wisdom, as well has his authorship of theological and liturgical treatises, he died in May 804 while still in post as abbot at the Tours monastery.

Even though it is agreed he was abbot at Tours, there is some dispute about whether he was actually a monk or not. Some historians suggest that he was, in fact, a member of the secular clergy at the time.

One of his legacies is the large number of letters he wrote, which have provided a valuable source of information about the history of his time.

St Alcuin's life is celebrated on 20 May.

Ghosts

It is claimed that York has more than 500 ghosts floating round the city. It is hardly surprising that some of them populate York Minster, such as the elderly gentleman who attends services or the figure in medieval clothing who has been seen carving wood. But one story from the early nineteenth century is particularly intriguing.

Two sisters, with their father and a male friend, were visiting the Minster. The eldest daughter and the friend wandered off and were studying one of the monuments in the north aisle when they noticed a naval officer, in full uniform, walking towards them. The friend saw nothing unusual about this, but the young lady reacted by almost fainting on the spot. As he passed them, they heard the officer say quietly, 'There is a future state', before continuing on his way. The friend helped his troubled companion until her father arrived. He then went off to find the officer, without success. Later, the girl revealed that the officer she saw, and whose voice she heard, was her brother, who had died at sea!

Other ghostly apparitions include:

Roman soldiers at the Treasurer's House (but only from the knees up)

A lady in grey at the Theatre Royal

A Tudor lady walks through the walls of the King's Manor (now part of York University)

Among the many pubs reputed to be haunted are:

The Black Swan, which boasts three ghosts: a workman in a bowler hat, a young woman in a long white dress and a pair of ghostly male legs.

The Snickleway Inn, which is thought to be haunted by at least five spirits – including Mrs Tulliver (an earlier licensee) and her cat! There's also a young girl, an old man, a nun and an Elizabethan man.

Wartime York

York was bombed during both the First and Second World Wars.

There were three Zeppelin raids on York, all in 1916. The first was on 2 May 1916 at about 10.30 p.m. and although it only lasted ten minutes, eighteen bombs were dropped, resulting in nine fatalities and forty people injured. The commander of this airship was Kapitänleutnant der Reserve Max Dietrich. Further raids that year took place on 25 September and 27/28 November.

In 1942, York was one of the cities on the receiving end of what were referred to as the Baedeker raids. Baedeker were publishers who produced tourist guides and the cities to be subjected to these raids were chosen from them. The idea was that destroying heritage buildings would cause British morale to plummet. The two-hour raid on York began at about 2.30 a.m. on 28 April, killing over 100 people and injuring many more.

There was damage to the historic Guildhall, among other buildings in the city.

REMEMBER · THOSE · LOYAL · AND
GALLANT · SOLDIERS · AND · SAILORS
OF · THIS · COUNTY · OF · YORK · WHO
FELL · FIGHTING · FOR · THEIR · COUNTRY'S
HONOUR · IN · SOUTH · AFRICA · 1899 · TO
1902 · AND · WHOSE · NAMES · ARE
INSCRIBED · ON · THIS · CROSS · ERECTED
BY · THEIR · FELLOW · YORKSHIREMEN
A.D

THE ZEPPELIN RAIDS : THE VOW OF VENGEANCE
Drawn for 'The Daily Chronicle' by Frank Brangwyn ARA

'DAILY CHRONICLE' READERS ARE
COVERED AGAINST THE RISKS OF
BOMBARDMENT BY ZEPPELIN OR
AEROPLANE

Food and Drink

York ham is traditionally dry cured and matured for a minimum of ten weeks, giving it depth of flavour and a firm texture. It is traditionally made from the meat of the Large White pig.

York Mayne bread, known in medieval times, was described in a lecture given in 1878 about Shakespeare's era thus: 'But these and all others the mayne bread of York excelleth, for that it is of the finest flour of the wheat, well-tempered, best baked, a pattern of all others the finest.'

Kit Kats and Chocolate Oranges

These products were originally made by two great York chocolate companies, Rowntree's and Terry's (now owned by Nestlé and Kraft respectively).

Kit Kat first appeared in 1935, but was then called 'Rowntree's Chocolate Crisp'. In 1937 it was renamed 'Kit Kat Chocolate Crisp' and the concept of the 'break' was introduced into its advertisements. After the war the name was cut to 'Kit Kat'. 'Have a Break, Have a Kit Kat' was first used in 1957.

Terry's Chocolate Orange made its debut in 1931. Prior to the Chocolate Orange there was a Chocolate Apple, produced between 1926 and 1954. The company's price list of 1867 had 400 items, only thirteen of which were made of chocolate.

The Castle Museum has an extensive collection of items relating to both Rowntree's and Terry's, although neither of these great chocolate companies manufacture their products in York now as their factories have closed. However, there are still a few independent chocolatiers in the city.

And a couple of cocktails

A York Special consists of 2.5oz dry Martini, 0.5oz Maraschino liqueur and a dash of orange bitters. Mix and strain into a glass.

A Duke of York requires 0.25 shot grenadine poured over ice cubes. Add four shots of orange juice, and top up with champagne.

Here's to Your Health

Over the centuries, York has been home to a large number of hospitals – there were roughly thirty of them by the sixteenth century, and more have been built since then.

Hospitals these days are for those with health problems, but in medieval times they also cared for orphans, housed the poor and gave food and shelter to travellers. There were even specialist hospitals such as St Nicholas's, which took care of lepers. But the English Reformation saw the end of medieval hospitals attached to religious houses.

Some medieval physicians thought leprosy was due to tainted blood, resulting in treatments designed to purify it. One such treatment was a mixture containing gold; it was thought that drinking it would cleanse the blood and restore the body's humours. Other 'cures' included regular bloodletting, administration of a drug made with viper's flesh and other ingredients, or medication using mercury – which was often incorporated into various medical therapies. But the treatment most frequently prescribed was isolation, even from one's family.

Then the Black Death (Bubonic Plague) arrived in York, not once but many times. It appeared first in 1349, but returned five times over the next forty-one years, making its final appearance in 1390. By then York's population had plummeted to 10,000 people, representing a loss of one third of its inhabitants.

Today, York's health needs are served by both private and NHS hospitals and health centres such as:

York Hospital, opened in 1976 (replacing York County Hospital, which opened in 1740).

Bootham Park Hospital, founded in 1772, the building being completed in 1777; parts of the original Georgian building are still in use.

The Retreat Hospital, opened by the Quakers in 1796; it pioneered treatment for the mentally ill.

The Knights Templar

A few miles south of York is the village of Copmanthorpe, where the Knights Templar had a preceptory. They also owned mills, located below the castle in York, given to them by Roger de Mowbray in 1185. These were rented out for 15.5 marks. They held other lands in York too, comprising three tofts which the Templars had bought, plus another that had been gifted to them by Thomas Usam (an important resident in the city). Henry III gave them a further piece of land adjoining the mills and granted them timber for the repair of mills in 1231.

A preceptor at Copmanthorpe, Robert de Rey, and the chaplain of the Castle Mills chapel were accused of poaching in 1292 by setting their nets below the mills to catch the king's fish. Not much happened to them though, as they were still in post a year later.

At the time of the suppression of the order in 1308, their lands had swelled to include a messuage (a dwelling house with out-building and land), three plots of land and rent from a chapel.

When the Knights Templar's order was suppressed, King Edward II ordered a form of stocktaking of all their possessions. The Copmanthorpe preceptory was valued at £80 16s 2d, with its mills in York being worth £10 11s 0d.

We owe the superstition of Friday 13th being an unlucky day to the Knights Templar. On that day in October 1307, all the Templars in France were arrested on the order of King Philip IV, who had many of them burned at the stake.

The order introduced promissory notes, enabling travellers to deposit funds at one Templar preceptory and get their cash out at another. You could almost view this arrangement as a forerunner to today's cash machines.

The Guildhall

At the point on the Ouse where the Romans probably forded the river, there now stands the Guildhall, one of four remaining structures built for York's guilds; the others are the Merchant Adventurers' Hall, the Merchant Taylors' Hall and St Anthony's Hall. The first recorded trade guild was formed by the weavers in 1163, who paid the king £10 a year for the privilege; by the fifteenth century there were eighty different guilds.

The Guildhall was originally built as a joint venture by the city and the Guild of St Christopher and George in about 1449–1459. It was intended for use as a meeting place for the guilds. Shortly after completion, it began to be used by the council for their get-togethers.

During the English Civil War Cromwell enlisted the help of the Scots. That help cost Cromwell £200,000, which was counted out in the Guildhall.

In 1936 the building was due for repair to damage caused by death-watch beetles; the estimated cost was £12,000 and work was expected to take six years.

The Guildhall was bombed during the Second World War and received substantial damage.

In 1957, the decision was taken to completely repair the building. The cost was estimated at over £130,000.

Fortunately the stone walls were still standing. Local landowners donated large trees to replace the original wooden pillars which had been crafted from trees which had grown in the medieval Forest of Galtres, 6 miles north of York.

The restoration took eighteen years and was re-opened by Queen Elizabeth, the Queen Mother on 21 June 1960.

The Bar Convent

Open to the public, the convent:

...is England's oldest convent – it was founded in 1686 – and is still active with resident nuns

...belongs to the English Province of the Congregation of Jesus, an international community of nuns founded by Mary Ward (now on the path to being made a saint)

...has a pair of her shoes, reminiscent of today's 'platform' shoes, in their museum. Mary walked from Germany to Rome in them

...has a portrait of Sir Thomas More which probably came into the convent's possession as a gift from More's descendants

...has a lovely dome in the chapel which cannot be seen from the outside because, when it was built, Catholicism was illegal. Anything connected with Catholic worship had to be hidden, so the roof was designed to obscure the dome

There is an infirmary for ailing nuns needing permanent care, and a pastoral centre running courses on education and religion, echoing the reason the order was established in the first place

You can even have bed and breakfast here or a meal in their excellent café.

THIS·PLAQUE·WAS·ERECTED

Born in
Yorkshire

MARY
WARD

1585–1645

Foundress and
Educator

BY·THE·YORKSHIRE·SOCIETY

Merchant Adventurers' Hall

Today the Merchant Adventurers' Hall is a museum and one of York's most popular venues for functions – but it wasn't always thus.

In the past it has reflected the company's religious and charitable interests, as well as its trading concerns, just as it does now. This magnificent Grade I listed building is a scheduled ancient monument of national importance.

The land the hall stands on was given to them by Sir William Percy in 1356.

Building work started in 1357 and it took four years to complete the original structure, which stands above a former Norman mansion.

Timber for the new building was supplied from Thorpe Underwood, 13 miles north-west of York, in the form of 100 oak trees. Tadcaster, a similar distance south-west of the city, supplied 14 tons of stone, while the 20,000 bricks needed for the building were purchased from York's Carmelite Friars.

Further additions were built later, including the anterooms and the Governor's Parlour.

The present chapel was built in 1411, replacing an earlier one.

The charitable concern of the guild is illustrated very early on by its care of thirteen pensioners in the fourteenth century. In 1372 they were granted a licence by King Edward III to found a hospital/alms-house in the hall for York's poor; this was housed in the Undercroft for over 500 years.

Their trading business involved travel across northern Europe and as far afield as the Baltic and Iceland, buying and selling all manner of goods.

Today, the guild is known as a company. Although many of its members are from York's business community, it is no longer involved in trade. It runs the hall, administers its charities and grants and has a role to play in the civic and business life of York.

A Tour Around Yorkshire Museum Gardens

The Museum Gardens span 10 acres and many centuries of history. In 1828 the Yorkshire Philosophical Society received the land by royal grant to build a museum, now a Grade I listed building. It opened in February 1830 and Sir John Murray Naysmith designed its gardens.

The original conservatory, pond and small menagerie no longer exist, but some outstanding modern planting and design make up for their loss.

Among the many trees in the garden are seven Champion Trees, the largest examples of their kind in Yorkshire and between 80 and 150 years old.

The Roman period of York's history is represented by the Multangular Tower, which was one of a pair. A catapult would have been mounted on top, aimed at enemies sailing up the Ouse.

The lower portion of the Anglian Tower is possibly late Roman, but some authorities consider it to be a bit later than that.

Little remains of St Mary's Abbey, built just after the Domesday Book was compiled. Once it was a wealthy Benedictine monastery with a thriving community within its walls.

Those walls were built in the 1260s. They were constructed to keep York's citizens out during disputes with the monks over land ownership and taxes.

The abbey's atmospheric church ruins were sketched by J.M.W. Turner.

The ground floor of the Hospitium is medieval, but the first floor is modern. Originally it was probably either a guest house for people of low social status or a barn.

The remains of St Leonard's Hospital's undercroft can be accessed from the Museum Gardens. An earlier hospital on the same site was severely damaged by fire in 1137.

York City Knights

Founded in 1868, when they were called York Football Club, playing both association and rugby football.

In 1895 they bought the Waterman's Mission Hut in Fishergate for £85, which became their first grandstand and changing rooms.

In 1931 they reached the Challenge Cup Final for the first time.

In 1996, the club was renamed York Wasps, but financial difficulties resulted in closure in 2002.

Later that same year the RFL admitted the newly formed York City Knights to their National League Two, winning the league's championship in 2005.

In 2010 they won the Co-operative Championship One Grand Final and promotion to the Co-operative Championship.

KNIGHTS
YORK CITY

105

Battle of Fulford

2.5 miles (4km) south of York Minster is the pleasant suburb of Fulford. To see it now, you'd never guess that a battle fought here influenced the outcome of the Battle of Hastings a little over three weeks later.

On the 20 September 1066 an English army under Ealdormen Edwin and Morcar faced an invading Viking and rebel army led by Harald Hardrada and Tostig.

Not realising that King Harold was on his way north to help them, the English commanders chose to meet the enemy in the open fields and marshland at Fulford. They took up a strong defensive position at a ford immediately to the south of the village.

After many hours of fighting, outnumbered and outflanked by the invaders – many of whom were fresh on the battlefield – the English army retreated.

The *Anglo-Saxon Chronicle* and Norse sagas supply conflicting information about the battle and the numbers involved. What we do know is that when Harald and Tostig went to York to arrange terms and return of hostages, Edwin had made himself scarce.

Had our forces stayed within the city walls, the English army's losses would have been substantially fewer – the city walls providing good protection. Harold would then have had a much larger army to fight the Battle of Hastings and, who knows, William might have gone back to Normandy licking his wounds instead of being known to history as the Conqueror.

At the time of writing, the council wants to build a new estate on the site of the battlefield – which has led to disputes over where the battle actually took place.

Castles in York

Two castles were built in York by William the Conqueror: both were motte-and-bailey constructions.

The first was built in 1068. The second, of a similar size, was built a short time later that year on the opposite side of the river.

They were both burnt down in 1069 by York residents, so William had to rebuild them.

The Clifford Tower site building had to be rebuilt again in 1190 after it was burnt down during anti-Semitic riots.

Then it was blown down by a gale in 1228.

This was replaced by a stone building later in the thirteenth century.

It was rebuilt between 1642 and 1643, damaged in the siege of 1644 and repaired in 1652.

An explosion in 1684 ripped apart the interior of the tower and it was abandoned.

In 1700, everything except what remained of Clifford's Tower was demolished and a prison was built (now part of York Castle Museum). The castle is still a crown court where serious crimes are tried.

Today the castle is classed as a Grade I listed building and is a Scheduled Monument.

Royalty and York

King Edwin of Northumbria founded York Minster in 627.

King William Rufus founded St Mary's Abbey in 1089.

Edward I, Edward II and Edward III used York as a base for their various battles with Scotland. Edward I and III also briefly used it as if it were England's capital city.

Richard II not only visited York on a number of occasions, but also made it a county in its own right.

Richard III visited the city several times.

King's Manor, York was visited by Henry VIII with Katherine Howard. James VI of Scotland stayed at the same place on his way south to be James I of England; so did his son, Charles I who moved his capital to York.

Queen Victoria came once, but got cross because what was meant to be a private visit was turned into a civic ceremony. She had previously visited the Yorkshire Museum when she was still a princess in 1835.

George VI said that the history of York is the history of England.

Queen Elizabeth II visited York for its 800th birthday celebrations – which coincided with her Diamond Jubilee year.

111

Statues

Constantine the Great, declared Emperor in York in AD 306, sits outside York Minster gazing away from the great building towards the River Ouse.

A statue of the controversial artist William Etty, wearing a smock and holding a paint palette, stands outside York City Art Gallery.

On top of Monk Bar there are half a dozen stone figures holding boulders, as if ready to defend themselves by hurling rocks on invaders.

The three statues on top of Bootham Bar replace the original medieval statues and were carved in 1894.

There's a Native American in Low Petergate above a former tobacconist, his kilt and headdress representing tobacco leaves.

At the entrance to Coffee Yard in Stonegate there's a bright red 'Printer's Devil', indicating the site of a print works which was there until the eighteenth century.

Minerva reclines above what was a bookseller's on the corner of High Petergate and Minster Gates. One of Britain's earliest book groups met here.

There are more than twenty cat statuettes scattered around York on rooftops, walls and window sills.

Film and Television

Scenes were shot in York for:

Films
Elizabeth (1998). Location: York Minster, where Cate Blanchett was crowned.

Harry Potter and the Sorcerer's Stone (2001). Location: Pedestrian Bridge, York Station (where Hagrid gives Harry his ticket for Platform 9¾). Yorkshire locations were also used, including Goathland station, which featured in several of the films, as did Grassington Moor and Malham Cove.

Charlie and the Chocolate Factory (2004). York's Nestlé factory produced thousands of chocolate bars for the film.

Brideshead Revisited (2007). Location: Castle Howard, near York. Castle Howard was also the home of the Flytes in the earlier television series of 1981.

Television
The Secret Diaries of Miss Anne Lister (2009). York Minster was used as a backdrop for some of the scenes from this drama, which was also shot in some of the surrounding streets.

Crusoe (2008). Loosely based on Daniel Defoe's book, this series was filmed at Fairfax House, the Guildhall, St William's College and even on the River Ouse.

Lost in Austen (2007). Scenes were filmed in Shambles, College Street and around York Minster.

Eternal Law (2012). Locations: York Minster, Betty's Café Tea Rooms, York Law School's Moot Court room, The Gallery nightclub, Blue Bicycle Restaurant, Nuffield Hospital and St William's College.

York Racecourse has been used for scenes in *A Touch of Frost*, *Britain's Most Haunted* and *History Hunt*.

Jubilee Trees

To celebrate Queen Elizabeth II's historic 2012 Diamond Jubilee, the Woodland Trust invited people to plant trees. The Trust discovered that something similar happened to celebrate King George VI's coronation in 1937. The record they published showed the following efforts to commemorate the latter event in York:

In Rowntree Park: two chestnut trees, two scarlet hawthorns and a whitebeam were planted by the Lord Mayor and other dignitaries.

Members of the Parks and Housing Committees, together with tenants of what was then a new housing estate, planted 200 mountain ash and flowering trees on Lucas Avenue and Rowntree Avenue.

At Queen Anne Secondary School (now closed, but the site is currently occupied by St Olav's) the headmistress, Miss E. Netherwood, planted an oak.

At Gray Gables, Water End, a sweet chestnut was planted by the owner.

A Georgian High Society Home

Just a stone's throw from the Minster there's a striking Georgian mansion. You can't miss it – it's not called The Red House for nothing!

These days it is occupied by a large number of antique traders, but it was once home to one of York's leading social luminaries – Sir William Robinson. Prior to Sir William's ownership, the site had belonged to York Corporation who had purchased it in 1675 for £800 (about £70,000 in today's money).

At a time of social and cultural growth in York, Sir William was York's Member of Parliament for twenty-five years, from 1697, and Lord Mayor in 1700. He followed in the footsteps of his ancestor and namesake who had held the same positions when Elizabeth I sat on the throne.

Unhappy with the house which already existed on the site, Sir William had it rebuilt, but may well have incorporated part of the original building.

Occupancy of the house changed in 1740 when it was let to one Dr John Burton. It seems that he was the model for Dr Slop, the bad-tempered physician and 'man-midwife' in Lawrence Sterne's book *The Life and Opinions of Tristram Shandy, Gentleman.* Sterne's uncle had persecuted Dr Burton, which is maybe why he characterised Burton in a bad light in his book.

At the time that Sir William and Dr Burton occupied The Red House, it would have stood on an old narrow road called Lop Lane, which ran up to the Minster. Then, in the 1850s, the Corporation decided to build a new approach road to Lendal Bridge and agreed to extend it to Lop Lane; finally, the area in front of The Red House was widened considerably in 1860. The result has given us Duncombe Place and excellent views of the house.

Stonegate

As you wander along Stonegate, perhaps doing a bit of window-shopping, it's hard to imagine that Roman soldiers trod the same path before you 2,000 years ago. In their day, the road was called Via Praetoria and it now lies 6ft below the pavement you now tread. One of the meanings of the word *praetoria* is 'headquarters' and Stonegate leads directly to the Roman headquarters, where the Minster now stands. It remained a significant street in York's history.

Stonegate is so-called because it was the route used to bring stone from the river to build York Minster. Another possibility is that at one time it may have been the only paved street in the city.

During medieval times there was plenty of work for glass painters, as York's forty churches – as well as the Minster – all had need of stained glass for their windows. Stonegate was where most of these craftsmen were based.

Printers took their place. At the entrance to Coffee Yard in Stonegate there's a bright red 'Printer's Devil', indicating the site of a print works which was there until the eighteenth century.

That led to bookshops opening. It's easy to spot where one of them was located, as there is a golden Bible (dated 1682) hanging over the doorway.

Just off Stonegate, in Coffee Yard, there's a medieval house that was lost for some time, disguised as an office block. Dating from as early as 1360, Barley Hall was discovered when the offices were going to be demolished.

First opened for business in 1644, Ye Olde Starre Inn was once used by Cromwell's army as a pub and a mortuary.

A Dead End

Among those with some claim to fame and who are buried in York there are:

St William, York's patron saint. His coffin (a reused Roman sarcophagus with a modern top) is in the Western Crypt of York Minster. This area is used for quiet reflection.

There are several Archbishops of York buried there too:

Walter de Gray (*d.* 1255), enthroned in 1215. He was a favourite of King John, who had made him Chancellor ten years earlier. He was also important to the young Henry III.

Henry Bowett (*d.* 1423), enthroned in 1407. In 1417 he insisted on going with the army to fight the Scots. He was so old he had to be carried on a litter.

Thomas Rotherham (*d.* 1500), enthroned in 1480. Buried in St Nicholas's Chapel. Imprisoned because of his support for Elizabeth Woodville.

And a royal:
Prince William of Hatfield, son of Edward III and Philippa of Hainault. The only royal tomb in York Minster has been moved several times. It has finally come to rest in what was probably its original position – but not until 1979.

There's the great and the good:
William Etty (*d.* 1849). Buried in St Olave's Cemetery, Marygate, where there is a stained-glass window in his memory.

Joseph Rowntree (*d.* 1925), famed for both his social reform activities and his chocolate, is buried in York's Quaker cemetery.

And the bad:
Dick Turpin (*d.* 1739). He adopted the alias of John Palmer while in Yorkshire. His body kept being dug up, the first time by a labourer who took him to a surgeon for illegal medical dissection. He was finally buried in quicklime at St George's churchyard, Fishergate.

Some Last Facts

York's Lord Mayor always knows where his seat is at private dinner parties – there will be a silver chamber pot on the table in front of him. It was used by George IV and hopefully has been emptied by now!

The National Railway Museum has a lock of George Stephenson's hair: he's the man who built the first public railway line in the world to use steam locomotives.

When the Pope visited York in 1982, he said Mass for more than 200,000 people at York Racecourse.

Princess Anne, the Princess Royal, rode a winner at York Racecourse in 1988 when she won the Queen Mother's Cup on a horse called Insular.

In the reign of Edward the Confessor (reigned 1042–1066) York had 1,607 houses; by the time the Domesday survey took place in 1086 there were only 967.

When a monarch visits York, they have to stop at Micklegate Bar and ask permission from the Lord Mayor to enter the city.

Walmgate Bar has been continually leased out as a house from the Middle Ages until 1957.

In the 1995–96 Coca-Cola (League) Cup, Second Division York City beat Manchester United 3-0 at Old Trafford.

Picture Credits

Page